Twilight Roses

poems by **J.C. Olander**

Acknowledgements –
Various forms of some of these poems
have previously appeared in:

W.T.F., Primal Urge, Magnet Project – R.L. Crow Publications,
Convergence Journal, La Luna: Poetry Unplugged, CPITS Newsletter,
Lost Valentines Anthology, Imaginari, Poetry Now, Sex-Loves-Lies (CD),
California Poets in Schools Anthologies, Sierra Streams (CD), Iris (chapbook),
Nevada County Poetry Series Anthology, Sacramento News and Review,
Rattlesnake Review Anthology, Animal Tales (CD), Kiss of Death Anthology,
Grass Valley Union Newspaper, Lassen County Arts Council Magazine,
Hearing Everyone's Voice, Pinch Penny Press Anthology,
Mass Man Epiphanies (chapbook),
J.C. and the Apostles (CD)

Special appreciation to:
Judie Rae

Front cover photo located by:
Carol DeFord Heiderich

ISBN: 978-0-9971780-5-0
Library of Congress Control Number: 2021934657

RL Crow Publication
18454 Penn Vallry Dr., CA 95946
U.S.A.

Printed in the United State of America

Dedication:

To my teachers
who taught me how to compose
the poems in this book.

Contents –

Twilight Roses

Summer Nights Street Fair

Troupe al Ama Belly Dancers
jeweled crowd pleasers.
The young one stands out
studying technique, being pretty.
Back up, left, pose, smile – trellised
red roses encircling youth's bloom
richen afternoon sunlight falling
golden scene's reflection
coalescing mirror image
from dining room's three windows
Ike's Quarter Café, York Street side.
An all American princess
among roses, her eyes
golden blushed pears.
A diamond sparkles her belly undulations
jewelry archetype art – turquoise
chiffon skirt scarlet tassels flare
teasing thighs ancestors dance.
Gold coined hip shimmies
chattering light with choli halter mirrors
gold bracelets, anklets, ear filigree
ringing her skin an amber glow
garnets kissing her neckline to breast
passion her maiden cleavage.
A red rose opens
over her left ear in obsidian hair
falling to her pelvic
arched chakra knowledge
aligning body center balances
her ribs' elegant lineage
laughter catching crescent moon
beauty poised
in the café's windows
a rose opens
reflecting all that can be.

On the Way Home
for Will

Returning from the Yosemite poetry gig
LeConte Memorial Lodge
in sheer granite elegance
I drive the long way home
up through Teneya Lake Cathedral
meditation through Toulumne Meadows
Tioga Pass ice and the long
twisting precipitous descent to get down
onto 395 north – flowers coloring
eastern slopes yellow and green.

Cool spring cruising thunderheads
in my indigo 99 cruiser van
for this Sierra poet.
Lightning sparking
Antelope Valley ridges
coming through Coleville
slowing down in the high school zone.
Three girls and a guy sitting
mid-way on the entrance steps
the guy at the girls' feet
waiting for that final bell-ring.
Three beauties learning to let go
let their bodies ripen into wild women
they've been wanting to be
wearing short shorts, loose, airy
blouses sun light fills full
long hair shining halos
smiling at me.

Sixty-four year old grizzled poet
wind disheveled hair
bunched up in blue paisley bandanna
wearing fly-eye blue shades
a big grin hanging in the open window
just passing through
and the long legged, blonde girl
with curvy hips, tight in her pink short shorts
smiling at me, lifts up her left hand
flashing the victory-peace sign
and takes a good, long lick
on her red popsicle
the kind with the creamy center.

Yep! I bet she's graduating.
My, my, my.
Sure feels good
out here, on the road
no one sharing
my little poet victories:
the young, pretty ones
smiling for a little peace
just passing through.

Native Cypress

Three weeks hard rain!
Cabin fever sweats
couldn't take it!
Walked out into its drizzle
up Newtown Road side
into Macnab Cypress grove
stood under gray-green
fountains
clean, wet aroma
new year's first sunshine
over pine velvet canyon.
Deer Creek roars ...

Heavy Metal

In world's toxic
fallout
I visit the man.
He lives in the woods, five acres
wood frame cabin, winter warm.
"Back wood slacker," some say.

Hunter, tills soil, gathers edibles.
Raised the family tech world took
overdosing chemical pollution.

We discuss weighty words
open a bottle of spirits.
After a long hit
his brain brews a bit
then spits its juice, pungent
"Too many stupid fucking people."

I took a hit
from the bottle
fortify my nerves
for the swallow.

The Legacy

He grew up not
questioning authority – said
"Politicians got it down.
I do what my preacher says
is good to get to heaven."
He called it Leap of Faith.

He received a bronze star
with a bullet blessing his chest.
A few screams – killed him quick
leaping from the helicopter's door
sergeant shouting command
"Welcome to Nam. Get Down."

Fourth of July

After suffering a week
of grandkids' explosions
screaming, whining, damages
a healthy constitutional revived me.
Spotted the lot of them
huddling near the car
looking at maps, time lines
making plans for the week ahead.

I slipped into my Adidas
tight red, white and blue shorts
muscle Tee with stripes
fashioned pair of Patriot Pom-Poms
strips with silver star danglies
did a cheerleader routine
yelling
Go-Team – Go-Team ...

Café Mekka: Conversation Overheard

I told her, look, it's serious out there
they want to kill you
but do it slowly, taking
everything from you as you die.
She said, "You're over reactive. Quite
paranoid with a pessimistic outlook."

It's true! I said to her,
Don't you remember
Carlos Castaneda's Don Juan
running the iridescent night
chased by that black refrigerator
and the desert vine weaving up his thighs
around his torso – the white trumpets
blaring full moon pearl
from its pink veil's psychedelic cocoon.

"That was all make believe
and psychotic hallucinations." she said.
What about that witch spraying your office
with Black Flag, cackling about it
you were sick for a month.
"That was a cleaning woman
she didn't know what she was doing.
Besides, I'm a Multiple Chemical Sensitivity."

That's it, I said.
They come at you from any opening.
The refrigerator could be anything
a knife – a car on a lonely road
a disease picked up for love
or a kindness
at the wrong place at the right time
they get you and you're a goner.
"I'd hate to live in fear all the time," she
said, "worrying wherever I went."

It's not about fear, I said.
It's being aware – Here. Now.
Each moment's action
the responsibility.
"I follow my Book's Tradition,"
she said, "I believe what I know."

And what about that New Jerusalem
I said, the dust – living next to that
highway – human bombs.
You'll be lucky to get back alive.
"I do what I must do," she said.
Take care, I said.
Divinities help those
helping themselves and the others.
Keep a sharp eye.

A year later, nearing death
in chemical overloads, truck exhaust
pesticides, perfume of people
and their toxic plastic habits
she returned to heal herself
among mountains of her youth.
On a back wood road winding
through a forest in a cloud – smoke-dust
heavy with afternoon light's glare in her eyes
the refrigerator came for her
its door opened.

Alien Zone

Dead winter's night crackles tone
north of Needles' light zone.
Under Dead Mountains' shadows
asleep in our wheeled sepulcher
desert wind rocks our bodies in waves
whistle-horn – far away train piercing.
I'm revived in sweet scented gusts.
Greasewood limbs thrashing scraggly
leaves shake out drought's decade
praising its frenzy – six hours in a wet
dream rain dance with aliens.

I'm stepping out into this celebration.
It's chilly, mist sprinkling my naked flesh
pee on writhing dancer's bare limbs
entranced in their ritual's renewal.
Red, orange, yellow, white dots outline
horizon black night apparitions neon.
Trucks, high balling line to unload goods
on civilized desires at the Alien clubs.
I unload mine on greasewood roots
at outskirts of civilization in wild wind
naked elements in this desert storm.

Emaciated dancers praising wet gusts.
Piercing – whistle – train horn softens.
Further out, outline truck lights splice
black vault sky splashing my flesh wet
into greasewood frenzy
wet leaves seduce my naked body.
I open arms – holy water splashing me
numb-stiff in this desert's wet dream chill.
Emptied, I re-enter the wheeled sepulcher
lie down beside my loved one, drift off
in the wind's waves, sleep's renewal.

Bush Club

When word went out among the people
a selection awakened from the doldrums.
But the Administration lent ears
to Boss Man, rising his podium's form
twists weapons of Mass Destruction
like shrewd political revengers
for second short comings of fathers.
He snickers his plan to his ego's
members' clubs, beating their fists
on the regimen's comic terror table.
His character's mirror images
sharpen tongues for the drools'
emperor feast, heralding the applause
with squeals, grunts, snarling of teeth
igniting fervor's Furor.

The wretched hurt hungers for land
its nuclear field's rock-scape dust.
Its rough beast's fingers violate
the sacred place of the bodies
women and their children, hieroglyphs
entombed in a shelter's safety zone
their light ashen images baked on
concrete walls where Sirens scream
the great penetrator's fire ball.
Somewhere over Palestine, debris
falling upon the Home Land's Security ...

Southwest Clouds

Roil over dark ridges
of yellow pine and black oak
down Meyer's Creek ravine
flare sunset
across Mother Lode
chaparral choked canyons darken
amber glow fades
from Coast Range
the valley's buttes blacken.

Stuff crumpled paper
into stove box
stack in pine sticks
strike match
light paper
and three lamp wicks.

Add oak logs to fired box
shut door – clamp it
dampen heat.

Sit in stiff back chair
at table
scoot it up
centered in light
open – provocative book
turn pages
flavor richens
each word
chewed!
Kerosene flame
hiss.

Trickling chime melodies
leaf skeletons chatter
fall through rattle
in oak limbs
scatter in moon shadows
earth chews them
swallows.

Blow lamp light out.

Stand at window
quiet
in the dark.

Oak log ash collapse.

Crumpled voices
wind muffled.

Chime rings
bare oaks howl gust
flare of stars
clouds silver.
Geese
shadows in moonlight.

Skunked

How he told me
got me.
The whole stinking mess
garbage heaped up
cat food on his deck for the feral
forgotten lunch in his truck
behind seat over night
skunk raiding it all
stinking deck and house
scattering garbage everywhere
late for work, hurrying
banging truck up pot holed dirt road
he hadn't fixed for three years
didn't notice skunk behind seat
scared it to spraying cab
both bailed fast
stinking for a week.

How he had enough already.
Set out Have-a-Heart
trap – capture alive
its pungent stink in a clearing
among old growth black oaks
where sun beat down August
heat sweltering Kit-kit-dizzy
snarling its anger
the whole place stinking
its nauseous musk.

How it rattled the cage in the night
waking him from his dreams.
Its rasp gasp for water
in 100 degree heat dust cough
took three days to kill it
couldn't get close to its stench

with a twelve foot pole
dragged it away with hook and rope
buried the whole damn mess
in his neighbor's property.
Got rid of it all!

I had to think hard
on my depravations
trespasses I had forgotten
near life behind bars
ignorance of what we do
and do not do to others here
in the horrors of their lives.

On job sites
sanding wood and paint
spraying paint without a mask
in the wind drift – the toxic air
filling lungs with work's weight.
What good do warnings do
ignorance – lack of care – the hurry.
I didn't have a heart
to watch his lungs thicken with death.
I remembered the skunk
its claustrophobic breath rasp
tightening trapped pain
the last three days becoming earth
when the spirit bolts from its body
till peace remains
in old clichés
an eye for an eye, tooth for tooth
reap what you sow
what goes around comes around
gnaws my heart
bleeding tears in wild iris field.

The Rain Has Passed

The rain has passed.
Its mist
flickering
in pools
reflects
street light
glass in
night still air.

Nourishing Heat

Splitting cedar kindling
for quick fire starter
begin thinking on a woman
thirty years ago, lost
two teenage girls
and a six year boy in tow
hustling money and love.
I cut her wood two winters
stacked, dry, separated sizes
to quicken flames in her stove
showed her how it's lit
how to feed it
nourish its heat.
Happiness
warmth in winter..

Desperation Line

I was all alone
empty in my bones
so I walked by the station.

It began to rain
along came a train
so I climbed aboard with the wind.

We were rolling along
then I heard her song
saw her lick her lips and smile at me.

A little small talk
we took a little walk
to the rear of the train.

I was talking rhymes
riding smooth lines
and the sun was falling in the west.

We were flying high
through a starry sky
speeding together in the moonlight.

In the midnight air
blowing through our hair
she slid up-close.

She gave me a kiss.

Aurora Borealis – Nevada County

11/5/2001

The Big Dipper's tilt
pours Aurora Borealis'
scarlet cold brilliance
across our womb's northern sky.
Red-gold meteor streaks northeast
into our spiral mother's spine
piercing the dark void.
A black-winged messenger
flutters through blue oak shadows
acknowledging our presence!
Cygnus flees southwest
into the great slit
our galactic origin.

The Pleiades reply
a double edged meteor
into the-horizon
lifting the red night
into our bright cream
creation spirals
flowering stars.
Another winged omen
fluttering into myth.
A deep throated heart speaks
Who-Whoo-Whoo-Whooooo.

When the owl calls your name
the good book wisdom says
"You will see signs
the heavens will open
and a multitude of eyes
will greet you!"

To a Muse

When she breathes
my coals flame Wilderness
blaze Its dark heart's panther eyes.

'Tis but air's elements, you say? Ripened
drove Paris mad – plays upon this stage
poet stuff and such things dreams divine
on the shore roads to Athens – through Rome and on.

Aphrodite's ambrosial elixir
coursed our mettle's current – her rapture's
curse blessed this heart – christened
in a sparkle of dew – the glass sea.
The Dark Void – swirling stars!

The Mountain
for D. Levertov

Unemployed – summer in the Cascades
west of Goat Rocks
ten miles southeast of Ranier
lost in dense fog-haze.
Below serrated, rock ridge
on cirque shoulder
emerald-blue lake
scattered conifers.
I'm searching for firewood
following the outlet stream
into a clearing-slope-steepens
into golden fog sunset
heavy smoke haze browns skyline.

The stream plunging rock face
cascades' braids
forty feet splashing
dark pool
slashing forest canyon.
Cowlitz and Nisqually River Canyons
to Puget Sound in fog.
It's low tide
2000 feet and rising.

The sun's blood-orange globe
thickens horizon.
The amber distance clears
three vague ridge lines
bear northwest toward Olympus.
The stream's cascades brighten
fuchsia's efflorescence glow.
Out of the mist above me
the Mountain
rose in amber sky.

Evergreen College Run, 1978-80

Step up into bus
lurch forward
diesel exhaust sprays car
in rear window view.
Its window slides down
pale, mustached face
sticks out – signals
left lane shift – passing
road narrow here
up a slight hill and turn
through firs and alders
too late – face retches
car brakes swerves back
into jelly-like black fumes
head retracts with middle finger
up slides window.
He's coughing too much
pulls out of traffic.

I tumble coins
into collection
meter box
grab balance pole
swing into seat
in a weird – drone.

I smell sweat's
morning love
aroma finer than prayer.
I weep anxiety.

My skin twitches
squirms – sours
anticipating eight hours

in fluorescent spray's
job site.

Garter snakes stink too
grab one tight
it wiggles and bites
greasy, milk-like fluid secretes
stains shirts – stinks
wears away eventually
as matter dissolves.
Perhaps I need a career?

Red, white and blue bandannas
wrap frizzed hair.
Greasies are in style too
straggled, separated
limp, oily tendrils
slide on moist skin
brushed up plastic helmets
on mannequins.
Limp, cotton dresses
wool shawls and coats
drape shoulders, breasts
thighs – Evergreeners.

Stiff socks mold
moist feet – boots off
don't breathe – turn eyes
to pimple reddened face
tilted into open window's
stream of consciousness
sucking Mr. Good Bar.

Driver's cow-girl lover
recites Louis L'Amour
riding their purple prairies
accentuating rhythm's
leather saddle
humidity rising.
A woman stretches
armpit tufts flickering
breeze-softly
she rubs them with
her fingertips – knuckles
blinks repeatedly
sits up – perky tits
glances about her
pulls bell cord – kisses
her girlfriend wet and wild.

Sunlight flashing through trees
into open windows.
The rippling air rush
over muslin cream blouse
naked breasts, jiggling
child sucks.
Water rippling under bridge
we cross into city's fog.
I breathe life's sweat
bus slows – stops!
Door opens:
step on to concrete
in cold morning mist
escaping diesel exhaust.
Doing real work.
Surviving.

Tahoe – August

Deck planks
ripple up heat
along wood bench rail.
I meditate
in sauna sweat
watch grass field fade
hoppers chew'n stems
net catch'em.

They're crisp, nervy
slick
soft in fingers
too tight
ooze bitter juice
nasty taste
sticky air.
Through thorax – belly
hook'em good.

Grasshopper falls
into
Heather Lake
crystal flames
flashing trout
hooked good.
Filets
twenty inches
delicious cheeks.

April Coyotes

That's them. Coyotes, yip-howling
barking off the point, yapping-yarps
up Deer Creek Canyon stars – abstract
escape artists painting sky's score indigo
silvering chords into constellations.

Chaparral bards yelping zaggareets.
Quick survival analysts, tricksters
gunshot zeros, dodging bush-wackin'
sidewinders, ditching lagger wanna-be's
scratching out fence line riffs
pawing furry love bundles, appetizers
bunnies, hen-house layers, kittens
with eggs, garden green gourmets
oh-coyote mint flavorings please.

They're howling down the mush bawlers
worn out domestic dogmas, penned in
chain-link bluffers bellowing base
black cavities, canine decay, toothless
debris below the rock slope chaparral
gathering mosquitoes in their stink
doing routine for the master
teeth gnashing groan, transfixed
in doorway's blue eyed vision
the silver screened eye's glare.

But off this point's view, coyotes
are slicing ecstasy – night howling pearls
down Peaceful Valley fluff – teasing hair
laughing, breezy, cool, in golden-bronze
iris pool perfume – quintessential stars
thicken moon indigo – oh
keep your kittens in tonight sweet things.

Coyote's cat calling tallies, a hip-hop
hipster crossing rip-rap short cut, break-dancing
acid etched rock take five.

Doing coyote thicket twister
manzanita, ancient red limbs spiral up
out wild flames into stars.

Crescent moon riding Jupiter and Mars
Venus with Saturn and Mercury aligning
this great wheel's millennium.

In a circle of stones – in a larger circle
of larger stones and larger stones still
images in the flames' veil.

It's Coyote doing down time getting right
with the others roaming these wild night rendezvous
stepping up trick trail stone stairs high.

Coyote's howling good times
slinking down the shadow curvies
slipping in-an-out of bushy thickets.

In the garden's last, wild rapture
manzanita coals glistening – salmon steak
bubbly, sizzles grill – sea fresh.

Grilled a-la coyote yarp-howling
resurrection stars in the greening earth.
Blessing our body's gift.
Reverence its iridescent flesh.
Coyote snapping loose tongue chorales
wild eyed, yarling yarps from this garden's
red limbed flames leaping into night crystals.

Bush Birds

He's Bold! Commanding!
A Terrorist!
The bloody taloned
Red-Shouldered hawk.
Perched
way up top the old Gray Pine
Overlooking bush land
screaming
Kill ...

Denial

Sirens sing still
soul's fantastic lie.

Sharks gore its flesh
down black razor hole.

Twilight glimmers
white waves rush
rock – clash despair.

The crab climbs
to its naked vegetables
collects Mana.

Ah, Sylvia
we rage dark
nights howling.

Nights the waves
call our shadows
from its mist.

And yew trees
shudder
at cliff edge.

Nights its mist
denies what
we all sing.

Despair waves
on rock smash it.

With each breath
we suck from its sea.

Family Traditions

What sparked him was traditional
blind power forcing rigid
authoritarian creeds
proclaiming the patriarch's
"A Man's World!"

"Son, males are aggressive
be tough
don't cry or hug those boys."
"Eighteen and still a virgin?"
"We Build Men!"
"You all come on, ride out
to Marlboro country
where a man belongs."

And he rides on.

"I hereby sentence you to one year
imprisonment for the brutal
beating of the plaintiff."
"It's your responsibility to marry me
you're the father."
"Any male that's shamefaced, spineless
is a queer, a coward and
doesn't deserve to be called a man."
"I'm sorry—but the malignant lung
will have to come out or he'll die."

What got him
was a bull's eye in responsibility
a 38 caliber hollow point
blasting-skin-bone-brain.
"A man's world"
Oblivion.

What burned her was the lie
an un-surmountable assemblage
of congressional housewifery
a concentrated congestion
of the easy way out.

"Mr. Clean's nine week floor polish."
"Our spotless glassware
impresses the neighbors
dear."
"The only laundry soap with three cleaning agents
and deodorizer."
"The natural make-up
fashioned look."

And it rolls on.

"How many times have I told you
wipe your feet."
"Our neighbors own
a set of crystal
dear."
"Dammit
put your dirty clothes where they belong."
"You don't appreciate
what I do for you."

What got her
was rejection to recapitulate
responsibility's understanding
in becoming what could be:
the easy way out
insanity!

Motherlode Eyes

She writes "Darling please come."
She says wanting for me aching
watching north wind shaking
leaves from her
black oak golden canyon's
Motherlode eyes.

She's a woman wanting
fire from her home bound man
before the fall's frost comes
and the moon
light lying on her sheets
a lake of ice.

Says waiting for a man
is pain and sweating on a bed
for a dead child's birth with
the fire light
flaring rain wet glass
his naked eyes.

I don't seem to know her
when she turns from sunset windows
I can see her lips speak
but her eye's
flaring prisms paint my thoughts
with crystal light.

Says a man's got to love
to give his woman what she needs
when her eyes turn from
her mirror
wants her lover's lips wet
in the moon shine.

Says it bleeds from the soul
if a man's hunger ain't desire
he hustles up to pay
a woman
whispering to his money
"Keep me warm nights."

Doesn't really matter
what I write or say to please her
wants a man beside her
cause when chills
stab her naked body
she wants his heat.

Says the earth gives you sight
when its river flows in your blood
your spirit comes with love
let it live
and heal your body's pain
flowing from your soul.

Beyond Age

The desert knows and wind
replies in the grain of wood

thin contour – a seed husk, delicate
like fingertips touch brittle bone

in the cleansing hour wind
ripples over sand

beating feathers
a withered grass tuft whispers

sand shrouds shift
drift far into heat

atonement.

Indomitable

Rain

sprinkles

silver maple's

yellow

gold

brown

variegated

leaves

over gray granite flagstone

cosmos.

American River Bike Trail

Leave asphalt
for dirt road not traveled before
see what's round
San Juan rapids' bend
two deep, white curls
we rode in summer.

The dirt road
dips in a ravine
river on left
pool on right.
Salmon, centered
in one inch water
over road
flops heavy.
Stuck
splashing crystal
flowers rose
ripe, fall salmon.

Five to seven pounds
two feet long
shining flesh scimitar.
Fish out of water
I'll eat for a week.

I stop.
Watch it fight.
Weak losing life
unable
to propel its weight.
My hands
guide fish's glide
tail slap-dives it
into river's opaque jade.

Two fish in pool
water level lowers
rapidly.
Nimbus Dam Water Diversion Policy.
One salmon's generations
equals millions lost.
Food for thought.
The larger salmon
biggest I've seen
since fifties
red-black, white
fungus splotched
sluggish
slightly smaller fish
dark silver-red
jaws hook.

I splash in – Cold.
Ten foot wide pool
two feet deep.
Salmon round-up
splashing silver-rose
fish frenzy
corralling biggest fish in my arms
shove it onto road bed.

The other fish follows
grounding
heave it onto road
still struggling
push it into river – safe.

Navigate the slick, ripe
female, dripping eggs
easy forty pounds

three feet long
future's flesh
slips from my fingers
into the American River
recovering a generation's
taking of wild life.

Bridge – a Photograph

Where wishes fall from
big daddy's paunch held up
in three piece suit – neck tied
strolling over cultured antiquity
masonry stone work
he pauses upon
the arc's apex
at the present railing.
He looks down in the reflection
noticed at last in the eye's coins
rippling the dream.

In the deepest level of penetration
wondering what's below
the glassy, rippling surface
of the face staring back
in clear twilight – wanting
to see more than available
for the tightening hands
gripped on the railing
staring into blank space.
Between two faces
a shadow poles a skiff
over black diamond water
ripples approaching the man
in three piece suit
neck tied
centered upon the bridge
over the river dangling
on his life thread.

Borrowed Time

Here, in the crossroad's
Island of Golgotha
garden of time and space.

Kubla Khan sits satiated
in his pleasure dome
of stately manners.
Hypocrite ally.
Your reason unravels
the conundrum
see-none-are-dumb.
Plastic-coded eyes
have no sense to see
The Idiocy
teeth naked at last
buying birthrights
selling death rights.
There is no substance to extract
in the garden of time and space.

We chew our mercury lies
as savages spew poison
from their phallic wands.
Brotherhood squads
crush Wild Iris at dawn
as plutonium flowers' kisses
sweeten your body's ledgers.
Sorrow's synapsis
"Don't tell me, I don't want to know."
Oh, true bliss in the garden
of time and space.

Your time is my time
is our time and the water is
burning – burning – burning.

Teaching For Cal-Poets

In Rockbound Valley
blizzard howls snow at my tent
fluff up goose down – bagged.
Dawn light flares ridge pines
flute wavering with each breath
black oak sprout scarlet.
Ukiah pear trees
flower morning's light mist – ah
teach students haiku.
Gibbous moon brightens
Highway 20's great valley
bug guts goo windshield.
Smoke from
Yuba Gold Fields fire billows
up blue sky – blackbirds.
From the deep pond mud
frog fart bubbles up – pops
rippling the plop.
Aspen leaves falling
flutter in the breeze – August?
Oh, butterflies.
Who? Who hears horned owls'
wings ruffle through the black oak
gold leaves, falling – who?
Wind stripped maple leaves
whirling with snowflakes flurries
crickets singing still.
Two wrentits rustle
up toyon's red berry feast
too shy for scene – flee.

Driving Highway's Possibility

The wild, can leap up.

Other's world.
Deer! Smash.
Headlight's broken
bones bloody.
Clock work's
inevitability spins sensibility
narrowing
routine asphalt.
Even serpents
sacrifice their glistening cords
in the linear wheels' rhapsody
sliced!

True hunter's heart
knows key integrity
quicksilver nerves
energy field
landscape breathes
rippling
Mandala
spine quivers true
synaptic gap
connect.

What we wish
feeds knowing
quantum leaps
particle-chaos awakens
needles, leaves silken
among disciples
speaking tongues
through deer eyes
wolves' live
knowledge.

Mandala nerve
reverberates
forest zone
glows abstract
electrics
deer eyes deeper
filigrees connection's
true present:
image
passage.

Sphinx Moth Musk

August sears sunset
salt wet garments fall from our bodies
emerging from our dug out shelter
in the yellow-clay hillside's shadow
under century's blue oak
naked, the patio's flat stones cool our needs.

Lounging on pillowed linens
we indulge evening's primroses
opening golden – igniting stars.
The landscape dissolves
as night comes to us all.

Water's rush deepens
Deer Creek Canyon
darkened
the black oak leaves sigh.
Pine needles whispering up slope
into blue oak boughs
moonlight splinters
primrose perfume
our arms, legs entwine.

Darker brilliance
filigrees gold
stems vibratos
little castanets, crickets
chirping, lilting
serpentine sway
in young moon's curve
musk ambrosia.

Black delta shape
hovering
fans night visions

our pupils enlarge
eyelashes flutter
dark wings dart sphinx moths
gardening Dionysian tempo
whirling black mass electric
moon petals open
plunge tongue into honey dew.

Tahoe's Wild Things

I walk to market in the dark
for wine and tomorrow's
bread, milk, eggs
and coffee.
Kids in bed.
Wife's soaking in tub:
steamy – plump.
Our Friday night
rendezvous.
September – excitingly alive.

Cut down embankment
riparian meadow short cut
one-quarter mile wide wash.
Bright half-moon light, chilly
weaving between willows
practice Kundalini serpent sense
through six feet tall grasses
into marsh dark water
walking along a log.

Twist through willow branches
into log jam melody
silver ribbon swirls
deep moon shine, rippling
black, Cold Creek
splashing spooky
still night sparkles
walk-a-log shine across creek.
Wild cat and snake terrorists abound
in imagination let loose.
Take it all in
to learn the way.

Up embankment
sage brush into dense pine forest
shadows thicken, rocks, cold
pine limb spikes can poke eye out.
Walk slow into vault black.

SCREEEEEEEAAAAAAACCKKK!
Stabs terror into my heart scream.
Flat on the ground under sage brush scream.
Knife slashing flesh murder scream.
Serial killer monster on the loose scream.
Can't see anything – knows where I am scream.
Life's last breath scream.
Silent.

"For God's sake
what was that?
Where is it?"

SCRRREEEAAACCCKKK!
Rolls me onto back, pen up.
Defense against death monster.
In black pines above
wings unfold – a great shadow
sails into stars
wings as long and wide as my body
and the beat of the wings
breathing on my body.
SCRRREEEAAACCCKKK!
Vanishes into forest black
sparing me
a chance meeting
Death.

Her Presence

Perhaps the morning breeze
shuffling curtains
through the open window
or the scent of her clothing
down the stairs – out of my life
woke me.
I remember the cherry-blossoms
night air
lush curves she moved
arousing my fingers
to the body's needs.

Her presence
brightened my skin
still, in the afterglow
her memory's gift
her eyes – sunlight
glittering the poplar's
green-golden leaves' flame
in this mid-morning breeze
perhaps her hair – or linen sheets
caressing my nakedness.
Awake now.
I cannot remember if she is real.

Alone Chopping Veggies

Thinking of you
gone
the knife's edge
sharp
sexy, the way you split.

Then cut my finger.
Bad.
The one you loved
touching
your pleasure's
appetite.

The onion was too much
no
I didn't cry
but
the juice from the onion
stings.
Still does.

Graduation Day

She wanted benefits living together
sharing her space
perhaps lust.
Students of literature
single, a bit experienced
in sexual delights.

We would try it out for a year
then proposal and ring
to complete our terms.
Whatever it takes – graduate.
Why not?
She's comfortable enough.
We fit each other's needs.

She taught catechism
pronounce the mantra
"You are the most beautiful
woman in the world."
Her wine glass smashed reality.
Still, a bargain is a bargain.
But, the deal collapsed.

To ease the finals' tension
we shopped around for rings.
Her favorite colors, rubies
diamonds matched set
passion forever.
But, in spring's rebirth
a natural man from the sticks
I chose life's symbol of renewal.

On our live-in deal's anniversary
she opened the gift
"I've been jaded."
That was that – deal done.
I graduated, Master of Language Arts
and an eviction notice
to pursue my fortune's destiny.

Highway to Balletto

Sacramento, Stockton, Modesto,
Merced, Fresno, Visalia, Bakersfield.
Down Highway 99, all day through history.

The Great Valley
of California: San Joaquin, they have vanquished
your vitality, stolen your beauty, drilled their wells
pumped your oil.
Small towns, farms, dairies, motels, restaurants
bulldozed into four lane speedway, Agri-business
corporate takeovers dishing out fast food
fattening suburban population growth.
Trash flowering through Bakersfield, out Highway 58.
Tehachapi's – cruising curves up tortured
oak dry-scraped hills – leveling out – glide
through high valley pass.

Break out to Mojave's dry plains drought
grease wood, Joshua Tree skeletons crumble.
Darkness sweeping grit dust sheets
northeast up out of Boron mining town
digging up desert chemicals
filling our lungs with slag fines.
Traffic slows down – 20 mph
growls gears – full load freight truck twenty feet
behind squeals invisible brakes – autos hiss
and trucks swallowed in darkness, driving
blind, dust sheets sweep inclines into horizon's
1000 feet high – 80 mph winds
roil invisible highway, but we're going on
all the way out through Barstow.

Mojave River's dry sand headwaters to Soda Lake
dry dust baked – scoured.
Devil's Playground, sand dunes
swirling whirlwinds blackening the sky
swirling conscious fear into a handful of dust.

Turn off at Zzyzx Road overlook in sunset's dry fumes.
Nestle up van into a sheltered ravine, spared of wind's
dust blowing out Interstate 15 to Vegas. Crescent moon
hacking cut mountain range silhouettes. Wind's
fierce edge – cold, dry grit-dust air, scary in its wild
turbulence, shaking van's security. We could die in
this! How wild can it get? How Long?

Well, it's time for the Balletto: Zinfandel. We'll toast
the devil's dust blizzard blasting rage.
Ha, it's the zin that's in Balletto with world's fusion
music integrating ancient desert cultures into contemporary
mixed blends of America, soothing our fears
extreme archetype wind global warming, climate
change, too much population growth, what the hell
you want to call it. Rocking us into our sleep
all night – rocking us in space/time, in Balletto.

I Don't Get It

A buddy back in the day
had it all.
Food, sports, drugs
all he took in, burgers, steroids
hot sugar pies, ice cream, pork rinds
snickers, sodas.

I'd bum, beg, bet bites
before and after high school games
walking home laughing for handouts – a smoke.
Bob got girls too – gave him rides whenever he wanted.
Business M.A. graduate
sucking big gulps, canned cocktails. hotdogs, fries
fast food junkie, fructose high: white stuff
sugar companies deal cheap
teach you, keep you coming back
mass market media distributors looking cool sucking coke
chewing stuff, bragging techno trends, inhaling solvents
doing chemicals, meat sticks, crack
crunch carbohydrate trans-fat
scored in corner dispensary sales.

I never had money for it all.
Bummed, stayed skinny, hungry
wanting what I couldn't get.
It was all just too much;
I just quit wanting.

Diablo Interlude

Twice a week, she drives in
parks at a trail head
to Mt. Diablo
slips on her running shoes
takes off – running for the hills.
A mile away, twice a week
he drives in and parks
at a trailhead to Mt. Diablo
slips on his running shoes
takes off – running into open space.

They are feeling free
thinking of each other
hot, slippery
massaging each other's need
in a grove of low lying oaks
where a breath of wind
moves through the grasses
lifting the earth perfume
in the body's heat
whispering through oak leaves.

Sudden gusts of gasps.
Their moans
purring desire
in the rippling wind waves
over golden slopes
falling in the canyon's arms of leaves
out of the throat into suburbs
rustling the turning leaves
shading the homes where spouses
preparing the evening meal
for a late loved one
look into the trees' sighs
trembling the dying leaves.

Reptilian

Becoming aware of it
sitting at window
looking out over oak/pine forest
something below
draws me from the house:
a feeling
I am learning the
trust
of the land.

A breath of air
rising ravine slope
guides me down trail.
Hot August morning
red, raw clay/rock slope
blue, black, live oak
light/shadow.
Steps crackle slough
layer's centuries
thighs swish tall grass
scattering exotics farther.

I step between trunks
old live oak
in woodland/chaparral
odd angle
spirals
out from under
boot sole shadow
silk scaled braid

coils
patterned question
knowledge.

Eyes tunnel source
integrity licks air
intense heat
flicks fear rattle
heart head poised
our eyes fix.

Back up boot sole
a blue bellied lizard.
Still
on trail.
I am curious
twig tease
backs snake up left
in leaves and dry grass
three feet from lizard.

Poke lizard's life.
Test convulses nerves
propels body
quiver-slithering
down one foot slope drop
snake's eyes fix it
lizard arcs left
through leaves and dry grass
slither-quivering
back up one foot slope rise
last twitch stops
three inches from rattler's
flicking tongue fork
eyes fixed.

Returning
to the land's law
is the body's
purest work.

We hold that power
withholding the heel's bruise
out of harm's way.
Learn each other's needs
respect all
moving
over this land
since the beginning
when we first set foot
on this soil.

Twilight

Looking out from Grizzly Peak

Strawberry Creek's source

named for an extinction.

The bay area's populations below

their gleaming cities lighting the twilight

and the Golden Gate brilliance

The magnitude of their civilization

over – whelming.

The Rose

What joy
its petals opening
intoxicating bees buzzing
exciting senses
in perfume.

What heart ache
its petals falling.

Night Visitors

Jabbering quivering fetterrishes
of the screech owls
awaken us new moon night.
Third story French windows open
frame blue oak limb
balancing dark
over twilight's faint eye
two silhouettes
alight center stage
screech owls
at dawn's threshold
churdling fetterrishes in a skit
fluttering feathers with each fetterrish.

An amazingly laughable spectacle
or blessing: delicacies we provide
seeds, fruits, insects, perfume
evening primroses, sphinx moths, owls
in our garden's pleasures
feeding our dreams
waking us from our sleep
churdling fetterrishes in reply.
We two talk at two till
betwixt between
sleep seals a marvel
imaged in our brains.

In Reno, Nevada

Three itinerates sit
on a sand bank
among river willows
watch riffles
stars
appear with night.

"Hey!
Tomorrow we look for work.
Tonight we drink!"

Oakland Hills Looking Down

High in the Oakland hills
sleeping
among canyon conifers
woke up to pee

an
orange
crescent
moon
in

silver sheen bay
teasing the cities' lights
reflecting
its slide into an ocean.

Collapse

Rwanda's desperation
grabbed the machete
grind stone sharpened
sweat and blood
hacking steel:
"Gimme what you got."

"Look, you see that man over there?
He is wearing a pair of shoes.
Everyday he and his children
pass-by wearing shoes."

"I don't have shoes.
My children have no shoes.
I will kill that man
and his children for their shoes."

Monarch

Monarch – ephemeral beauty
gracing our presence in this garden
caterpillars eating our milkweeds.
Brief time span butterfly flutters
orange and black striped, white speckled tiger
like blending darker shades: lapis, purple
indigo flower cones flaring our butterfly bush.
Eternally fresh – beautiful flight
laughter from your lips into light
moves my humble gesture's praise
tears blessing Monarch passing.

Last flight – remember?
Flutters through the garden – gone
Monarch – was so –

9 –11

No news
with morning coffee.
I sit on flower bed's rock wall
watch birds flutter-hunt
drink in rock pool
splash-flutter-bathe
garden's pleasures
a.m. sun thins blue oak
shadows manzanita
toyon, coffee berry
lighten breeze talk.

Flash-rose. Iridescent.
Brilliant black feathered throats
electric green hummingbirds
two, exploding sunlight at lips
of morning glory blue petals.
The male juts back – hovering, rising
slowly, dazzling faster-higher-dives
invisible
Puuuuummmmmmmmmmmnnnnngh ...

Appears eye level
at three feet – hovering.
Its needle beak tilts left
black onyx eye
flares white star
stares into my eyes.
Straightening needle beak
zeroing closer it
arrows to cana lily's orange
towering stalked flowers
to sip honey dew.

Backs out – rising slowly
undulating up-quickening
into bird brained euphoria fall
Puuuuummmmmmmmmmmnnnnngh ...

Far away, across the continent
two silver-gray metallic missiles
rise from man's divination
stalk a flight path terror – plunge
its towering throats' veins
to drink a fiery martyr brew
flowering our nation's wealth
exploding vermilion-orange
black, oily petals
unfolding at lips
of smog blue sky
brilliant before
eyes' devastation
crumbles to
ground zero.
Terror rules.

Rock Terraces' Blessing

Topsoil created by earth each year –
4 billion tons
amount lost to erosion each year –
25. billion tons –
World Watch---S/O 1997

Rock work
two walls
three feet high
eighteen yards long
terraced garden beds.

Three years laboring
soil loss off our
thrust rock hillock's
east slope – it splits
Peaceful Valley down north
slope of Deer Creek Canyon.
Three rock runs to finish
be dirt rich.

Collect rock where you find it
high grade – glove gripped
carry or roll rock to pickup truck.
One-third to fifty pounds
one-third fifty to ninety pounds
one-third ninety
to one-hundred fifty pounds.

Lift or roll rock off truck
wheelbarrow to positions at wall
lifting, rolling, sliding
in – out – lift – placement.
Some stones lifted ten times
to fit good.

Tools
hammer, chisel, shovel, mattock
shape sense, clear sight line
taste determines.
Freestyle
underground solid block base run
stack them as you get them.

Drop set dry
rectangular, rounded
top and bottom flat
one and two foot wide rock
up to foot thick, granite
tie stone course
chisel chip notch
toe-in, pressure pinch
back slant batter, plumb
concave wall
with heavy, narrow, long
rock pins and wedges
chink out
clay pack
back up
with two-handed cobble
blockish, triangular
pound rock chunks tight.
Syntax
metal/stone ringing.

Centuries
rock stacked on rock.
Five heavy stones
set solid:
seven hours.

Sky's hair glows gold, rose-lavender
storm shapes angels
over Sierras.
Cold gust – raindrops
golden oak leaves swirl
veils down ravine
earth darkens.
View up Deer Creek Canyon
nine miles east
over Peaceful Valley
three ridges
town and houses in folds
10,000 people – vanish
in conifer, oak, manzanita
century's re-growth
in heart of Motherlode.
For a moment
alone in this forest
cloud heavy
twilight thickens silent.

Honking. Her-Honking. Her-Honking.
Geese rising from Peaceful Valley ponds
hidden in the darkening forest
honking continuously, louder, rising
over fall's gold filigree of black oak leaves
a thin line of rowing wings
between tall, gray and yellow pines
golden in sudden sun shaft
gilding thunderheads
arrow of seven Canadians
beige, white, black piercing
the gold veil of mist
showering this garden's
stacked stone.

Summer Nights on Grunt Hill

Toads bungle and bend trails
through stiff, straw weeds
content acquiescence
hunt lacewings
that lap up aphids.

Cicada "clicks."

Acorns bang shingles!
Fall through manzanita
to ground leaves.

Coyote barks
far down slope
dogs bawl protest.

Jerusalem cricket slides
under empty brown paper bag
and fidgets.

A baby longlegs
learns its mobility
manipulating its stilts.

Claws scratch concrete
dog sighs.

Crane flies buzz
fly like
in drunk flight
their stick frames
flicker in lamp light
and shadows
flicker on oak leaves.
Stars fade into dreams.

Roadkill

Driving up Harmony Ridge grade
Hwy 20 east. Sierra tourism.
Confusion backs up car issues
diesel trucks blacken air's lungs
around turn, slow, inside curve
downhill lane stopped – deer in ditch
kicking hind hooves, furious – broken front leg
plows chest, jaw, antlers up embankment.
Above road cut, two does, at dense edge
of canyon oak re-growth, gold rush cut.
We watch seven people, out of two sedans
three SUV's and log truck driver, fresh
dead Doug fir load in racks, gnarling face
in cab, as they watch buck fall, roll down
embankment – regain power – churning
hind hooves, push chest, sliding up gutter
channel's Tertiary mud flow rock
Harmony Ridge – ten thousand years
lineage in this deer climbing these slopes
into summer forage at the headwaters.

Would a bullet to the head do good?
What feelings wash memory clean?
The two does turn from the scene, bound
up in the slope's green-silver shadows
comfort canyon oaks provide. Log truck
belches black, driver yelling in cab
as more trucks, cars, back up grade's
curve, tourists continue watching
writhing animal's death dance.
Our windows rolled up to the
oily air as our line passes by.
What else can we do here, but foul air
watching life's death dance finale?

The Hunt

That rat
gnawing nut shell
roils sleepless agitation.

Peanut butter and chocolate
Cliff Bar
stuck in rat trap's trigger trip.

Will crush it.
No guilt.

Keeping the Dead in Place

We pulled out the institutional crab grass
weeded family plots, swept plaques
trimming, cleaning each monument
raked soil and scattered seeds, violets
buttercups, lupine, poppy, phlox, flax, coreopsis
baby blue eyes, owl's clover, farewell to spring.
Seeds gathered throughout county, sowed
mixed in with organic soil and leaf mulch
foothill mix richened – packed – watered well.
Leaning on rakes and shovels into evening
talking sun down below pines in fiery clouds –
winter storms on the way.

Did subversive middle age activism
a four week stint clearing project's
bureaucratic nightmare red tape run-around
conforming to governmental permits for
authorization to supplant the caretakers'
death cult ritual: spraying poisons over
Pine Grove's antique head stone cemetery.
Perhaps want of dead for the dead.
Whatever. In Nevada City Cemetery?
How about celebrating spring renewal
planting flowers Nov. 1, Day of the Dead.
Earth nourishing Earth.

Seeds took – nudged up sprouts – life
all over in new year's greening haze
coloring stone memorials in distinct hues –
moving light through pine – cedar – fir shades.
February – caretakers returned equipped
with tools of their ways: negligence
cross communication, ignorant stupidity.
Spraying poisons keeps the dead in place.

Madison Ave. Blue

I saw them
I saw them last night
while riding my bike with no light
walking arm in arm along the avenue
aged lovers strolling a full moon's gold rise
pause by a fountain – shadows
between street lights
embrace
one to another
clutched
in the light beams of auto after auto
after auto streaming along the avenue
between street lights
and fountain
shadows
in stars
glimmering
in haze.

Angelic Harp

When the Angels' harp
strings sing true
age improves
the instrument's tone.

So many years laboring
marriage familiarity's
mundane necessities
quick step dancing
to keep it together.

When we embrace
and I slip my hands down
inside her tight fit Levis
squeeze firm buttocks
Snap – strum her panty strings

heaven's harmonic quickens
her secret angel fingertips pluck
the muscles – pure tone.

To Questers

Leaving ancestral homelands
on the move – searching for the path
to renewal's fertile soil – again plant
seeds – enrich Earth opportunities
raise strong wise sons bearing fruit
bright-eyed sagacious daughters
new roots rooting deep minerals
stamina in the soil's sacred promise
nourished in their field's vital substance.

When harvest feeds the family's love
generations brought forth celebrate
inhabiting the land's fulfillment
a healthy body – mind discovering
the garden's green lit solitudes
communing each other's laughter.

We will arrive home
with what we now own
bodies, minds and hearts
wrapped in each other's arms
blessing our light.

Live today tomorrow's peace
germinate community knowledge
each and all understanding
voices singing the harmony
our children's intelligence
generations of bright stars
illuminating path ways into night
the silent bridge our hearts beat
at last – we arrive home.

The Babits

January cold – cut firewood – clearing
manzanita, oak, buck brush, dead, dying wood.
Fire spring chills into summer bar-b-ques.
Bow saw catch – rip-cut-flesh-deep – bleeding.
Stitches – it's hard, dangerous work: joint-twist
fall-rock-gash-stick jabs – trip into forever.

How fortunate, 75 years, working muscle's
precision to useful body brushing fire lines.
Scars teach me well – I'm ready – splitting
rounds with maul and wedges passed to me.
Still, intent fires energy, true heart each season
doing it – forty years escaping BABITS.

The Boys Are Back In Town Scene – the crowd.
Jim, cool, heavy, heroin OD at 19. Fritchi riffed
guns and drugs for a Duel Prison brain operation:
quadriplegic – doing 15 years in Demerol – done.
Herbie, Jerry, buddy system, shot from copter in Nam.
Chase butchering the neighborhood kids with knives;
his hatchet struck fear into our suburban hearts.
Big John, Elvis look-alike, 20 year's old, car washer
left his wife and three kids: 38 slug-exploding-brain
forever. Jerry and Gary twins, chain-whipped teens
into a man slaughter prison sentence forever.
Flowers swore never again prison, but punked out.
Roger, sniffing paint, glue, gas, burned mind
clear racing I-5 into the white light stream forever.
Dennis speed-needling pig shoot-out to kill himself.
Jack, Tracy, Sean, Louis, lifers touring the big joints.
Tracy says, "Give me 500 bucks. I'll kill'em for you."
Richie sang the names: made the hit list – disappeared.
Stan, Larry, Fred, drowned in Early Times whiskey binging.
Sammy and Curtins drove little girls to bad news forever.
Rick, biker president, speeding diabetes on the edge

crashed it all over cliff. Brother Skip playing devil
dealing fire card stud, lost heart in smoke and mirrors.
Beer cap biting Mike's heart attack chugged him, 37.
Gerald's 40 year tobacco habit heart attack: a striper
pulled him into the Sacramento River forever.

How it all could have been different – or could it?
And the old cliché, "Only the good die young."
Buddy checked out, bullet; Brian, Gene, Dave, the noose.
Tom and Bill filling lungs with paint, dust, solvents working
trades – cancer smothered lungs before retirement pay off.
And the others: immune and organ disorders and failings
cell disruption, the corporate toxin pollution, drugs
bad and no choices, guns, government policy rip offs.
Fathers fist beating psychic put downs, dead beat slap
across the face, kick him down, "I'll whip Ya good."
Ripping flesh with belts, sticks, rods, whips, fists
"Ill toughen you up – Be a Man!"

All I can think of to do now is care, precisely.
Splitting rounds with maul and wedges splits
open the past: choices back then—when into
present: working on survival, a few goods
pleasures, well-being, construct rock wall terrace
food garden---steel chisel singing true stills
heart tone—flowers future: pruning trees, move
plants, rocks, set stakes, burn fire break rings
seed and marry land's life—this woman and I.
April breeze sprinkling rain into sunshine
to get it right, nourish us all the way through
believing it's all good.

Maxim

At the filling station
Paiute Casino, Bishop, Ca.
I witness "Baldwin Effect."
Two Brewer's blackbirds
a pair – patrol parked cars
filling up with fuel
inspecting each car's front end
to flutter up – pick off
insect carcasses splattered on grills.
Ah, Olander maxim
first sign of intelligence
ability to adapt to an environment.

The Work

Barking – coyote
yip-yip-howls
down slope
manzanita thicket
under oak
canters up
toward me
bow sawing
log rhythm's blue oak.

Fall evening
twilight.

I lean in
to oak trunk
shadow under
golden bough
flaring myth
passing
black tipped
toes, nose, tail, eyes
define its shape.

Remembering Lewinsky

Suddenly
not knowing why
on her knees before all that power
she had ever believed was true
passion swelling between her lips
her teeth clenched hard on
the bullet!

Laid Off

Tuesday morning
second hand swings up
sunlight fills house
through windows
blinds never close.

It's time to get up
feel the air
our muscles – stretch.

But first
let me feel
your arched back
and buttocks
firm – cool
gripped
thighs – warm
silky like
your wet hair.

We got time
you better take it
it won't last long.

Rising for self-employment's
a low incentive
with this compensation thing
coming in.

Looking for Beauty

Where Highway 20 meets
Big River's N. Fork
hike up logging road.

Steep, narrow canyon curves climb
into redwood's second generation
huge for minds
don't know old growth.

Sun spears
mid-morning dark shade
dappling shadows
spotlights a sweet spot.

Five royal purple-rose iris
fan from tuber's fins
young sword fern
center-spews
six lime-green fronds
catch light shift.

Above all, tall straight
thin tube stem splits
horizontally arcs one-third circle
eleven finger-like fronds
with wavy edges
symmetrically lengthen inward
centering its thrust
toward light.

In the understory
large, three leaf clover
variations in green fluff
lavender-pink five petaled stars
sprinkle it pretty.

Bottlebrush horsetail
half-circle border into shade
golden pastoral still life.

Mosquito whines into light.
A blue-silver dart
damsel grabs it.
Alights on leaf point
between wild iris
bites mosquito's neck off.
Eats head
thorax
abdomen.
My blood.
Discarding crumpled wings
and the exoskeleton
darts elsewhere.

Below the iris
under the clover's canopy
on the redwood-needled earth
ant enters clearing
red with large black head
hefting a squirming maggot
captured from a dull feathered jay
crumpled to earth
outside the light's arena.
In the tangled forest's omnipotence
raven croaks three times.
We return to where we began.

This Instant

If I could hold you
melt through your skin
muscle – bone – to your marrow
become one with your soul
would I know you any more
than what I know of myself
the instant
our eyes mix.

Prayer Flags

She hangs out prayer flags
to April's blue sky breeze –

A string of multi-colored butterflies
her silky panties –

Petals fluttering perfume into sunlight
from our garden's multi-colored iris –

I can't help it
sniff the prettiest –

Buyers

I like my neighbor:
no pets, noise nor nosy.
Wants to sell out since wife split.
He's got the buyers from the bay. "Yea.
They're going to stop by and tour the place.
But I might not be here when they arrive."
He says and tells me,
"It would be nice to meet your future neighbors."
"Yea!" I say, "Let them know what's here!"

Walking the line to catch their drift
we meet up – they're sold
but the buyer family's wife
wants to know
 "How safe for our cats?
White fluffed Persians."

"Not good!" says I
"When they go in the woods
something happens to them
lose sense, stray too far
killing birds, snakes, lizards, insects
feeding hawks, eagles, coyotes, rats
hunter becomes hunted."
She winces
her face twists down
distaste for what's to come.

"Yea!" says I, "Could be raccoon
coyote or eagle eats'em
sometimes cougars snatch'em off the porch
or a bullet gets'em!"
That was that!

They bid good-bye and drove away
smiling and waving at my neighbor
driving up smiling and waving back
dreaming done deal.
And that was the last time
my neighbor mentioned the buyers.

Noon Tide

I've seen her before
here at the docks
her sun-tanned shoulders
her blonde curled locks.
Brush in hand.
Pen in hand.
Paint with oil.
Paint with words.
Though we never speak
here at the docks
we portray our scenes
the eye unlocks.
Far apart
we sit
together
interpreting
it.

Winter Solstice

In the longest night
of new moon's ice.
Awake, I
lie in my bed
alone
cold!

Woman with Flowers

Diego Rivera's Lily Lady kneels
her head lowered as if in submissive prayer
to accept the weight carried in a woven basket
wider than her body, hefted upon her back
by the man behind her – this world's beauty.

You notice his thick hands
grasping the basket's braided rim
his large feet on the black earth
straw hat tops the white flowers.
You could say the lilies' essence
rises from her shoulders' strength.

Attached to the basket, a blue sash
binds her stout arms at the shoulders.
Her hands clutch at its taut knot
heart shaped, centered on her breast.
The sash's strands fall between her knees.
She holds the vein blue cross at its crux
reciting daily her rosary's mysteries.

She wears a beige triangle fringe shawl
like a holy tunic of her order, over
the long sleeved black dress habit.
Perhaps she is praying for a blessing.
Perhaps for enough money to continue
tomorrow's burden of human suffering
upon her body's wide, sturdy back.

White callas on green stalks
vessels from the black flesh of earth.
Count thirty-nine lilies in the basket.
Maybe more with a bit of imagination.
Lucid, white heart shaped callas

golden phalluses piercing erotic needs.
All lines balanced symmetrically
to support the painting's weight
upon the heart.

Vernal Equinox – 2003

Waking from a restless sleep
rain pounding the roof all night
into morning's cold, crystal light
feeds spring's first signs of life.

The bombing has begun again.
All night bombs have been raining on Iraqis.
How many tens of thousands of women and
children under the power of men's might
will die for this spring's sacrifice?

Soon, the Mother Of All Bombs may fall.
Have we become completely crazy?
Where's the metaphor in this reality?

At times, I am ashamed to be a man
wanted to be a woman, bring life from my body.
"Teiresias! Can you tell us what we should do?"
I know women kill too, with spite, greed, arrogance.
At times I have been ashamed to be a human being
wanted to be a beast roaming the forest for needs.

This cold morning is that time.
See, even now, with the sun, shining,
clouds rain tears on our human deeds.

Concerning Global Warming

If you listen
to an inconvenient truth
you will hear
the answer
there's money to be made.

Working in the Castle

I stood next to the King once, 1975
working in Sahara Tahoe Hotel's
concrete dessert paradise.
Warehouse lead man – in the basement.
I push the button, 11:30 pm
the dock's door rolls up
in under world's iron curtain racket
in rolls pearl limousine: Cadillac!
Windows black – I close the door.
Exhaust smoke thickens concrete cavern.
A brute body guard in blazer and slacks
steps out into soft black fumes' dispensation
opens the rear door.

The King steps out
white scarf, black leather blazer
white ruffled shirt, frilly cuffs
linked in silver and diamonds
black pants and white shiny shoes
removes his shades, winces
in false light of lingering spent fuel
pulls off black leather gloves
left hand first – relaxed.
White, creamy skin, dough-plump.
He looks sharp – but a bit too done
extends right hand and a jeweled beauty
emerges, luxurious in fur coat matching
gold-blonde-black-streaked long hair
rolled up and loose
black stiletto heels, meshed black nylons
short black tight skirt catches pearl glimpse
when her thighs open to step out.

They smile at each other.
The King lets go of her hand

and looks around.
Pans his snicker pout, does a groove move.
She slips her delicate, tanned fingers
silver tipped jewels
under his arm and he leads the way
up the stairs to the ramp
as a kitchen boy pushes
a wheeled iron vat, 2'x 4'x 2' deep
food scrap soup, five vats a day
along the ramp to the dump bin.
Did he notice the King
pause for him to pass?
The King walks past me
I nod and smile.
The King smiles at me
his signature recognition grin.

I want to poke his ivory skin
would it spring back vibrant like a god
or stay depressed like dead fish skin.
But his lady's smile
catches my eye as Elvis passes.
But the brute is way too close, too wide
and much too serious demeanor.
I step back quick out of his way.
All three move through the kitchen
elevator up to his private room's door
where he and two brutes
fist and kick beat a drunk
near death a few months before.

Now, the King returns
to the scene of the beating
redeem himself – settle the score
for a slight sum of money.

I push the button
the iron veil rises
and the pearl, black window limousine
backs out – turns, glides away among stars
over the lake.
The kitchen boy returns, slop cart empty.
I look him in the face
for recognition of the King's passing.
He sighs, nodding at the empty vat
"Wasted! Money and food. Wasted."

J. C. Olander, uses musical images, personal experiences, sounds, phrasings and ideas to blend performance and spoken word into an "Action Art Poetry." He is a Poet/bio-educator with Cal Poets, and is the current Poet Laureate of Nevada County, CA (2019 – 2021). He has taught poetry and recitation in/at elementary and high schools, colleges, rehabilitation institutions, festivals, conferences, and privately throughout the West and beyond. Olander is a Poetry Out Loud California State Champion Poetry Coach. He is a long time organizer and featured reader for the Berkeley Watershed Environmental Poetry Festival (Poetry Flash). He regularly performs his poetry with dancers and musicians. His books include; "River Light", Poetic Matrix Press, 2017; and Twilight Roses, R.L. Crow Publications, 2021. He is an organic gardener – gifting most of his yearly harvest to the local food bank.

Made in the USA
Middletown, DE
01 April 2021